A WORD LIKE FIRE

Selected Poems

D1384255

A WORD LIKE FIRE

Selected Poems

DICK BARNES

Edited and with a Foreword by

Robert Mezey

HANDSEL BOOKS

an imprint of
Other Press • New York

Production Editor: Robert D. Hack
Text Designer: Kaoru Tamura

This book was set in 10 pt. Sabon by Alpha Graphics of Pittsfield, NH.

10 9 8 7 6 5 4 3 2 1

Library of Congress Cataloging-in-Publication Data

Barnes, R. G. (Richard G.), 1932-
    A word like fire : selected poems / Dick Barnes ; edited and with a foreword by Robert Mezey.
       p. cm.
    ISBN 1-59051-167-0 (pbk. : alk. paper)
    I. Mezey, Robert. II. Title.
    PS3552.A695A6 2005
    811'.54–dc22
                                            2004015844

CONTENTS

from GRANITE INTRUSIVE

I

Born in San Bernardino on November 5, 1932, Dick Barnes lived most of the first fifteen years of his life in what he referred to as "the wilds of eastern California," first in the tiny village of Running Springs in the San Bernardino Mountains, where from earliest boyhood he fished for native trout in Deep Creek and carried in the wood his father had chopped and split for the cookstove, and then for some years in small towns out on the Mojave Desert. Beginning his education in a one-room schoolhouse, he continued it in high school, first in Barstow and then in San Bernardino, and at Pomona College, Harvard, and the Claremont Graduate School, and went on with it until the day of his death, May 15, 2000.

He was a quiet, affable, humorous, and generous man, deeply loved by his many friends and his wife and children. Some of his friends, naturally, were professors and fellow poets, and some were cobblers, doctors, carpenters, musicians and barflies. He was a devout Christian, and a Taoist—neither a common thing in colleges these days—and, rarer still, a man of great humility. I never saw him lose his temper or heard him raise his voice; he was one of the few people I have known that I would call enlightened.

I don't mean to imply that he was some kind of saint. His wife burst out laughing when she read that bit about never losing his temper—like most of us he had to deal with powerful emotions and no doubt he expressed them in the privacy of his house, in the intimacy of a happy marriage—but he was remarkably tolerant of and courteous to his colleagues, even the most foolish and exasperating of them, and I cannot think of one who did not like him. He and I worked together translating the complete poems of Jorge Luis Borges—twelve years of the closest collaboration, the frankest give-and-take, and sometimes passionate disagreement—but never once did we quarrel.

He was a man of many talents, and in addition to his career in scholarship and teaching he distinguished himself as an editor, translator, dramatist, filmmaker, and jazz musician. He wrote and produced well over a dozen plays and what he called fire-operas, elaborate dramas that featured music, fireworks, and giant puppets, staged in the midst of immense landscapes—a butte and a dry lake in the Mojave, a ruined winery in Cucamonga, an abandoned quarry in Upland—works of startling originality, some more successful than others but none that did not leave the audience glad that they came. He edited a number of scholarly books and anthologies, he made four films—comedies, collages, and a vivid visual and musical accompaniment of poems translated from Wang Wei and Li T'ai Po, the originals chanted by Ch'en Shou-yi; he translated widely from Anglo-Saxon and Spanish and Italian, and he played washboard and sang the blues for many years in the Real Time Jazz Band, the songs mostly his witty and poignant rewriting and refashioning of old standards.

But poetry was the fixed star around which his life revolved. His knowledge of it, of all literature, was extraordinary, both vast and intimate. He had studied the Latin poets, he had taught himself Italian to read Dante and Provençal to read the troubadors, he had read widely in the literature of many other languages, especially Spanish and Chinese, he knew folksong and blues—indeed, he seemed to know every poem in English, from the earliest carols and riddles to the various schools and pathologies of contemporary American poetry, not to mention the efforts of the aspiring young writers he gently taught at Pomona for nearly forty years. His specialty was medieval and Renaissance literature, but he was probably the only member of the English Department who could have taught every course offered. As it was, he did teach a great many—Anglo-Saxon, Chaucer and his contemporaries, Dante, Tudor and Stuart poetry, Blake, Joyce, erotic and mystical poetry of Judaism, Christianity, and Islam, the biblical and classical backgrounds of English literature, silent comedy, experimental film, Ozu, Bresson and others, sacramental theater, the peculiar activity they call "creative writing," and more. (He was also deeply knowledgeable in the sciences, especially astronomy and geology, and in mathematics.) His classes tended to be small—he must have seemed rather formidable to some students in spite of his easygoing, good-natured disposition, and then too, not many students nowadays are dying to learn Anglo-Saxon or study Chaucer or Dante—but I sat in on three or four of his courses and thought him a wonderful teacher, learned but not puffed up in his learning, sympathetic, full of insight, sometimes very funny, and always absorbing.

As a poet he was patient and hardworking—"The lyf so short, the craft so long to lerne"—and he developed slowly. I think he knew from early youth that poetry was his calling, but he said to me once that it was many years before he began to feel confidence in the quality of his work. Unlike the myriad poets who start fast and soon fade, he kept on, dissatisfied but undiscouraged in the face of almost total neglect, discarding, revising, translating, making new poems, while steadily improving and growing into a distinctive style of his own, one capable of a wide range of expression but without mannerism, ostentation, or whoring after novelty. By the early '80s, some of us thought him one of the most original and powerful poets writing in English.

He has an engaging variety of subjects, and to all of them he gives faithful perception and love. He is partly a regionalist (albeit of a not very fashionable region), a nature poet of uncommon lore and the tenderest observation, but he also wrote love poems, satires, song lyrics, elegies and panegyrics, poems of wry social comment and occasionally anger—his anger all the more lacerating for being expressed with such quiet restraint—and devotional poems of a very high order. I sometimes think of him as essentially a devotional poet, though the devotion is rarely obvious and never pious. He can be wildly funny and heartbreakingly poignant—sometimes both at once. Some of his pages are as oblique and hermetic as, say, Paul Celan, and many are as simple and direct as the Scottish ballads and the blues. He was interested in everything and he rarely wrote a poem that did not seem to arise from some deep necessity.

Any editor who asked him for poems received a sheaf of them, and over the years he published hundreds, all but a few in ephemeral and half-forgotten mags. Many were gathered into chapbooks, half a dozen of which were published, or I should say, self-published. His two full-scale books, where much of his best work is to be found, were issued by very small presses in very small editions: *A Lake on the Earth* by Momentum, no longer extant, and *Few and Far Between* by Ahsahta. In his last months, he recorded most of his poems on a set of eight CDs, readings of great strength and delicacy, interspersed with apt comments and good stories. (Anyone who would like to obtain them should write to Patricia Barnes at 434 West 7th Street, Claremont, CA 91711.) At his death he left the typescript of a substantial new book, which he entitled *Granite Intrusive*.

That his work was not very widely known seemed not to trouble him, at least outwardly. He must have been hurt at times by his exclusion from the more prestigious journals, which regularly published poets who could not hold a candle to him, but he never uttered a word of complaint to me. He certainly knew, because we told him, that several of his fellow poets considered the smallness of his audience a scathing comment on our present literary culture. But if he had comparatively few readers, he had very good ones. He could count William Stafford, Peter Everwine, and Donald Justice among his admirers. Miller Williams said of him, "More than any other poet I know, Dick Barnes makes poems out of what he sees in the backyard next door and what he comes across walking home from school. I can imagine giving his poems to a visitor from a very different world in order to give him a sense of who we are." And David Ferry wrote, "Dick Barnes was one of the best poets we've had in America. Why he wasn't better known (except to other poets) is a mystery to me. His poems hold the joy and grief of our common experience up together, to look right at them in a radiant light. He speaks the purest mother English in his poems."

Wherever I open Dick Barnes's poems, whatever line my eye may light on, I am drawn immediately into his world. It is, of course, a world made of language, like anyone's poetry. But it is also a humane and coherent world made of experience, of long and serious thought, of profound feeling, and, always, of the wakeful and generous consciousness of a particular soul, whose song can be heard in every line. That is *not* like anyone's poetry—hardly anyone's. A current flows through it from poem to poem, making itself felt as much in the syllables as in the design of the whole. It is something that cannot be faked. In "Up Home Where I Come From," a poem about a hawk that has been accidentally caught in a trap and brought home by the trapper to be fed and healed, Barnes writes:

> *There in his basement, in a hutch built for rabbits,*
> *it glared at us with its unfathomable eyes,*
>
> *accepted the dead meat he brought it, even hamburger,*
> *unquenched. That wildness*
>
> *is what we can know of dignity.*
> *We aspire to it ourselves but seldom—*
>
> *seldom. Nailed to the tree*
> *Jesus must have been as still as that,*

> *as wild. And I'd say*
> *that was the right way to be, there.*

This is exquisitely characteristic of our poet's diction, moving easily from *hamburger* to *dignity*, accurate and convincing in every word—nothing for show. If you try to cut a few words or add some, or change their order, you will see how strongly these lines are made, how pure the writing, for all the ease and plain-spokenness of the voice. When I come to *but seldom*, I wonder for a second if the rhetoric is not perhaps pitched just a touch too high—but no, that second *seldom* immediately disabuses me. It shifts the grammar slightly—*but* doesn't mean quite what I thought it meant—and the timing of that repetition across the couplet break makes my pulse jump: it is like an arrow striking home. And who would have expected to find Jesus in this poem, and so justly, such a "sudden rightness." The cadence is equally characteristic, sure-footed, full of little surprises, perfectly adjusted to the flow of thought and feeling.

These poems are almost all in "free verse," the most difficult kind of verse to write, and utterly unteachable. Every line gives pleasure to the ear and to the organs of speech. Metrical phrases and lines appear, sometimes a lot, sometimes a little, but naturally and subtly, like the rhymes, which are often internal, sometimes assonantal, usually occasional, but used with telling effect. Listen:

> *. . . pyracantha berries neither green nor red,*
> *the yellow poplar still mainly green, the green*
> *of the gingko dimmed, that will change to bright yellow*

> quick as a traffic light, sycamore, ash, persimmon,
> peach,
> summercanopied yet but with fringes fallen at their
> feet . . .

My impulse is just to point to poem after poem—"Few and Far Between," say, or "Clearing the Way," with their gorgeous place names, Miltonic in their sonority but deeply American, and like honey on the tongue:

> through Essex and Cadiz Summit, great tamarisked
> Chambless,
> Ludlow for breakfast with the humorous Chinaman,
> Lee,
>
> Newberry Springs, Daggett and Elephant Butte, Nebo
> hidden by wire,
> on home over the hill to Barstow on the good road.

Or "Dusk Was Falling," Frostian in its sympathy and diffidence, the first half of the poem very simple and ordinary, nothing special, until we begin to realize what is at stake and all those ordinary details come back to mind now haunted by wordless woe. Or "Every Man His Own Cross"—a painful poem, but the pain lifted (in Frost's phrase) "to a higher plane of regard." These are some of the things that being American means—some of the better things.

Or look at "Example and Admonition"—one sometimes sees this kind of completeness in really good metrical verse; in this mode, where one is absolutely on one's own, it is a small miracle.

My father's admonition: when given
a choice, choose the path that
leads uphill, always,

so up we went, but all led down soon after:
our destination Deep Creek, where water had gathered
by taking every downhill opportunity.

We thought of that when the higher path turned down,
but no one mentioned it then, nor ever, in fact, til now.
Two lessons, and though sometimes I feel clever,

and have read the Chou I book all about that water,
I've not forsaken either one. If there be something in a
    man
that flows uphill, he has to go with it

whatever sweat or humiliation may attend his going.
Done patiently, this is called "matching heaven with
    heaven."
Otherwise, just strife.

The movement is thrilling: the three short, blunt, prosy lines, and then the rise of a clear and spacious rhythm, borne along as it were by the pentameters—five, possibly six, in the next nine lines. Dick Barnes earned the right to work in this mode by mastering the old craft, which rewarded him by refining what must have been a naturally good ear until it was a marvelous one. Not many have it. Listen to the verse of "A Word Like Fire," one of the most moving devotional poems written by an American in this century, maybe in any century—to my mind it is better than anything by Taylor or Very. Its epigraph is from Jeremiah, ch. xxiii: *The prophet that hath a dream, let him tell a dream.*

> *In my sickness I withered from one shape*
> *to another: finally I was a little dry spider.*
>
> *The doctor put me down somehow into two holes*
> *in the wet sand, and went away. I was to wait there*
>
> *until I got well or died, when the sand dried*
> *and caved in on me; that would be time for my*
> *   resurrection*
>
> *in this life or the other. What is the chaff to the wheat?*
> *saith the Lord, Is not my word like a fire?*
>
> *saith the Lord, and like a hammer*
> *that breaketh the rock into pieces?*
>
> *Jeremiah wept to say it, but I find*
> *I still have some eagerness for this experience:*
>
> *the doctor goes away but the Lord*
> *goes down with each of us into the grave.*
>
> *That was my dream, and I am afraid*
> *but have taken a dare from Holy Writ to say it*
>
> *and may the name of the Lord, or his billion names,*
> *be praised, I shall praise them for ever and ever.*

I knew what it said, only it seemed incredible,
not anything you'd want to say out loud

in this world, that has its own enervating problems
with their own ineffective solutions, its detestable hopes

that are like hopes I have myself or have had
(they come away like the nail from the quick);

is that what it's like to be naked: nailless, eyeless,
given to visions, aflame: and what a cool breeze then

flows like neutrinos through your empty spaces.
I have felt it like clouds of them billowing through.

The laws of verse are not immutable, any more than the laws of our country, but like them they are rooted in long tradition and precedent, and only a true poet can bend them with impunity. Nowadays the poets drop in and out of meter at will, or more likely by accident, not recognizing the measure; but ignorance of the law is no excuse—off with their feet. Dick Barnes mixes free and metrical too, but he always knows exactly what he is doing. In this poem nearly half of the 28 lines are pentameters, strict or loose—the two cadences move in and out like silk. I see that I keep coming back to the sound of his lines. I am reminded of Pound's famous dictum that technique is the test of a poet's sincerity, or, even better, Donald Justice's line, "a love that masquerades as pure technique." But it *is* love—both the ground of technique and the transcending of it. Attend closely to Barnes's verse and you will come to know his heart. His heart is pure, he tells us in one poem, and it is—we trust this voice because the rhythm doesn't falter, the words ring true, have the sound of truth—unmistakable.

He has other virtues, too many to list, but let me mention a few. As I have said, his range of interest and subject matter is very wide. I love his poems about the natural world, which he sees with clarity, gratitude and reverence, but without intrusion. Unlike most poets, he isn't concerned in the least with what we think of him: what he is concerned with is his subject and the art of getting it right—in this, he is like Hardy, and Herbert. And he also does what Confucius thought poets should do, among other things: teach us the names of the plants and animals, and instill respect and reverence for the natural order. Even the phrase "natural world" isn't quite right. As in the Chinese poets, as in many of his poems, it is the world of sentient beings, including us; and more than that—the clouds and rocks and rivers are equally a part of it, and they seem sentient too. Not a Peaceable Kingdom, to be sure—just the world, beautiful and cruel. Of course, he sees clearly that unlike the other animals we seem not to know how to live in this world very well. Like Frost, he looks at our urban civilization with the canny eye of a countryman and he tells us things we might never think of by ourselves, or not in that way, but immediately recognize as true. Gentle rebukes to our blindness and ignorance. Little tales of the ignored, the humble and enduring. Moral epiphanies, but utterly free of the odor of sanctity, the wagging finger of the preacher.

A lot of his poems are about work, and he truly knows what work is. He comes from people who worked hard all of their lives, he himself works hard and loves work: he sees its beauty and dignity as well as its tedium without sentimentality or special pleading or humorless resentment. And when he writes about workers, about the oppressed and the outcast, it is with seriousness and fellow feeling but without the slightest self-righteousness—he is not using them for his spiritual pleasure or for cheap vatic thrills or for basking in his own virtue. "Pomona Laundresses," "Trophy Hunt," "Rakestraw Coyne and Boyle," "Alfalfa," "Clearing the Way"—these poems don't require that you do anything; there is nothing you *can* do but wonder and understand. You can call them political poems if you like, but they go far beyond politics. Read his elegy for "Willie Boy." Is there a more searing poem about the misery and tragic fate of an American Indian? If there is, I haven't seen it, though there are many Indian poets and many white ones who have taken Indians for their subject. I can scarcely bear to read it, it is so unsparing and so merciless. The mercy is in the mercilessness. It makes me think of his little poem, "On a Painting by David Hockney," which ends:

> ". . . . *There it is*
> *exactly, my cunt of a life.*"
> *In case you thought it was so easy being*
> *a Beverly Hills housewife.*

Plain American "that cats and dogs can understand," so plain that you might not notice the elegance of the lines, which end with something rather like ballad measure, or the rhyme on that last, normally unstressed syllable that elevates it nearly to the loft of a metrical accent—the same thing Hardy does in the last word of "Channel Firing." One could say that it is the technical mastery and ease that lift the woman's bitter regrets to the pitch of silence and assent—to a higher plan of regard.

There are many sad poems; how could there not be, in this fallen world, the way we live? There is "Thin Ice," a wry little parable that gets all "the woe that is in marriage" without ever saying a mumbling word about it. And "Big Ed," a sort of *vers libre* sonnet, a brief, tough-minded elegy for which the word "sad" is not nearly adequate; it's also rather funny, and praiseful, defiantly so. And Barnes can be abruptly hilarious, as in "Shoot Out." Who else would think to meditate on Niels Bohr and Western movies and turn it into a religious poem, one so oblique you don't realize that your head has just been cut off? A good many of his poems are religious poems, but like this one, not so you'd notice, not until you stopped laughing.

He has qualities we tend not to demand of our poets these days—a keenly observant eye, profound learning worn lightly, wit and good humor, a feel for the *mot juste*, a deep knowledge of life that even at its bitterest has not at all diminished a childlike capacity for wonder at it, and the willingness to tell the truth as he sees it, wherever it may lead. Nor does it ever occur to a reader to ask, Why was this poem written?—it was necessary, obviously. And *we* needed it. In one poem, he says, "Wisdom is wisdom, / help is help. Didn't you know that?" True enough, but sometimes wisdom *can* be help. Poetry too is sometimes a great help, when it's as good as this. Think of "Example and Admonition"—the wisdom is not the kind that can be packaged neatly in a precept or two. The example seems to contradict the admonition, but the speaker has "not forsaken either."

There seems to be a narrative, but it doesn't come to much: we are told nothing of the group or even why they are in the mountains; the paramount drama is "where water had gathered / by taking every downhill opportunity." (John Ruskin would perhaps have condemned that figure as "pathetic fallacy," but I would give a great deal to write that well.) The strength to take the path that leads uphill must involve a willingness to go down too, in fact, to seize the opportunity. You can meditate on that a long time without ever quite getting to the bottom of it, but clearly it is no mere paradox or trick of words. Or think of the candor and humility of the sick man in "A Word Like Fire"— sick unto death, and yet what a joyous vision he experiences, in spite of his prudent fear of saying so. We may not have had such a vision, we may even doubt its significance, but we cannot doubt the honesty of this man's confession. How can we not be persuaded by the tone and clarity and rhythm of his sentences, his cold regard of the world's "detestable hopes" and immediately his unvarnished confession of having had the same hopes, and above all, the metaphor of the breeze enclosing the stunning simile of the neutrinos in the final couplet? What amazes me is that a man can write as well as Dick Barnes does and not be renowned for it. As Bum Phillips once said of one of his great players, he may not be in a class by himself, but it wouldn't take long to call the roll.

I spoke earlier of gratitude and reverence; let me end with that. It seems to me that those are notes not struck very often in contemporary poetry, and we are the poorer for it. We hear much more grievance than grief, more discontent and cynicism than praise, more self-aggrandizement than humility and acceptance. (I believe it was Margaret Fuller who said, "I accept the universe," and Emerson—or was it Carlyle?—who said, "She'd better." In any case, Dick Barnes said it too.) His last book, *Few and Far Between*, ends with a poem called "Bagdad Chase Road in July," and the poem ends with these lines:

> *Thank you, rain, for flavoring our jaunt*
> *with a hint of danger, and for the splashy mist*
> *when you lashed the desert hills to show*
> *what you can do when you mean business.*
> *Thank you, other twolegged bare featherless creature,*
> *for sharing the jagged horizon of my life.*
> *Thank you rainbow over the East Mojave*
> *low to the ground so early in the afternoon:*
> *thank you for being here with us.*

Yes, thank you. Thank you, Dick Barnes, for being here with us.

Robert Mezey
Claremont, 2004

A LAKE ON THE EARTH
(1982)

Lynx Rufus Showed Me the Way

Lynx rufus showed me the way and vanished
down a dark grove without a trace
the leaves listened even they couldn't hear him
there I was in the dark, and where I stopped
an inch from my face
suddenly a great yellow spider big as a hand, her web
must have spanned twenty feet from oak to oak

she there quite still feeling the taut line
to know what was happening

all the sounds of the night

I went in then but beyond the ping
of my bare bulb I could hear them out there
for an hour more or less, and danced
all the way down over the chaparral canyons and hills
covered with buckthorn and sage to the trains
hauling through Lordsburg loads of bombs and oranges
whatever it was they carried
and sang and nothing was changed

Hatauva

Benjamin Morongo saw the place
where the corpse of Kukitat was burnt to ashes
the circle around it where the people were dancing

(to this day the coyote looks back when he runs)

covered over by water now, the dam
water I fished for bluegill bass and crappie
once took away my ring, a brass ring
that would fit any finger and decode radio messages

down into the water rayed with light

slap slap of wavelet against the boat,
the rowboat, not knowing the god's pyre was under us
under the lake

The Longing of the Soul for Absence

The purity of the air, its aridity:
so many came here because of t.b.

or just for emptiness itself, the "desert"
Sinai or Canaan: naked sons of Ham

think of the Lao-tsu book
think of the Alcoran

the railroad, the roundhouse, loads going somewhere else
broke down or out of water; Malleys coming over the pass

all that is past, but you still see it
in the lawns, or along driplines between new houses

that longing for loneness, the vast empty West
wild miles of just weeds and the trees along the river

out by the air force base, austerity
of Galaxy Circle, Liftmaster Place

a BB gun by the back door
instead of a fence or hedge

no place to write home about, no one around, space
strafed by the sun, scoured clean by the north wind

Rakestraw Coyne and Boyle

He held in his hands
a sticky, stinking, meagre mess,
one briefcase full, but greed told him
there was something in it: the resonance
between his own greed and someone else's.
It was a billion billion easy rides, happy landings, safe sex,
a new occupation for the Indies, fountain pens, blimps,
    combs,
gramophone records, a short job of work for Bertie Rodgers,
fake flesh, toy tractor treads, sockets, we'll never
in our time see the end of it, it was
rubber seeds but he didn't know it
all he knew was it was worth something,
a lot, to someone else, somewhere else, and so
greed took him to California
in his quest for a certain, hidden, exploitable need
when he had what it took to fill it.

Survivors Along Poplar Street in San Bernardino

In a mortuary or musical comedy
pink light doesn't fool anybody.

We sat in piano recital chairs
while a young bland employee of the place

praised to the heavens Aunt Lizzie's exploits as a Christian.
He never knew her at all so he said too much.

She was a plain poor woman of no distinction
except (as he forgot to mention) she was dead

which is why we were there, but under that light and what
    he was saying
we all looked deader than she did.

It took my grandmother, afterwards, leaning over the coffin:
"Well, that's the road we'll all be going one of these days."

The neighbor ladies in their print dresses
fluttered like so many flowerbeds in a breeze.

Now praise.

Being Careful Back Then

"Never drink from the water glass you find in a hotel room:
some old guy probably had his false teeth in it all night

like the one you hear now
coughing through the wall."

When my parents and their friends were young
that's the way people thought about germs

and Jimmy Bostwick—
well, he had to stay home from the Orange Show

so many germs were there:
and wouldn't it happen, he was the one

who came down with mastoiditis
and died first of us all.

They bought him a hat
to wear in his coffin, where he'd been cut.

His parents—well, do we ever
get over anything really,

however nimbly we learn to limp:
pain can teach us a new dance every day.

My mother went for a few weeks to stay with them—
old friends, close friends.

My father was considerate too: when he phoned her there
he said "You can answer this question yes or no:

how are they?"

Alfalfa

Past midnight in a wide field:
out there a John Deere tractor is stalled.

By the light of a drop cord
an okie and an arkie, two rednecks are working

from sunup. They both are tired,
their movements have become unhurried and sure.

One says, *They're all sposed to run—*
that's what they're made for.

Knuckles barked where a wrench slipped hours ago,
the treachery of rust, grease, worn metal, fatigue.

Well don't that go to show—the dumb
resistance of a machine. Arcturus sinks

toward the horizon,
autumn stars gather in the east,

a breeze lifts dust
from the half-harrowed field. They keep on.

In their leisure they are violent
intolerant men

but now in the night when I hear them
their voices, that courtliness, that calm concern

I too lack social consciousness
and I care nothing for anyone's scorn

The Time of the Tumbleweeds

My father watched the scar where the fire was
in the mountains above Redlands for years

and he was the engineer who had the idea: where
    tumbleweeds
grow along desert highways the state

can let them alone. Buicks coming back from Las Vegas
will have to take their own chances

with shapes rolling over the freeway; the sand
blows over it too and no one aspires to get rid of it:

some hazards will remain no matter how prudently
the authorities provide. He came out against guard rails

along curves on mountain highways: "If they can't
steer well enough to stay on the road

let them fall off, then they won't
bounce back into traffic and hit somebody."

Early one morning he lifted back specimen tumbleweeds
green and still moist with the scant dew of the desert

sure enough there in that shelter and condensation
a new world was alive, the bunch grasses

the flowerlets that grew up after
that could take hold

while tumbleweeds having lived out their era
left roots and rolled away in the wind.

It's practical just to let that happen.

"At Barstow"

Midway through the Sixties the English poet,
Charles Tomlinson, was benighted in Barstow,
California, that used to be my home town.
He had his car refuelled, he took a quick walk and
a look around: he had a taco at a taco stand;
then being a rather tired poet
stayed overnight at a motel.

He remembered the air, how he could smell
the gasoline; he heard big trucks throb in the night;
he remembered how neon looks from afar,
yet to him it seemed a placeless place,
not European and at the same time
not English; to him the North Star
seemed lower than it ought to be;
he didn't speak with someone, and though
he read reports of his four senses
he didn't notice much. Memory and fancy
eked out with irony, he composed
a poem for his fans: "At Barstow."

In the morning
up rose the sun, and up rose Tomlinson,
and on he went.

Tomorrow the world.

Not His Fault, His Misfortune

What ought she to do, stretch
credit indefinitely fiscally, neglect the state
and get away with it, sell you
a horse blind of an eye?
Sing you a song and a half about cocktail
brides, about angels (a fat lot she knows)
and if she sets you up you'll like it,
that warmth of credulity, that wild swoon of assent,
you'll never know what hit you but she knows.
O she is a poet but there's more to it
not true to it either but absolute
in that most any moment
shameless yes as Eve was in Eden, but conscious, in
imagination, like memory's mint, to stamp out just
any thing she likes, to say it
and to make you think it
my god just to be able
to lie like that.

A Song for Charlie

A year pretty much since Charlie Stivers died.
I'll sing you a song he wrote, that Sue Hertel
sang at his funeral, so you'll know him:

I was standin on the corner, lonesome as I could be
when a very ugly man stepped up and tied his horse to me.

The vodka is in the freezer, immune
from that cold: I pour myself another
thinking of how Charlie died of alcohol.

He'd call me on the phone and tell
a story he'd made up about the two drunks
or a sadder one about the lonely drunk: our songs!

It wasn't liver trouble, it was straight
poisoning: the hard way. He lay naked
on the floor in his kitchen, in a pool

of what his lungs gave up when he died.
Pat Frankel found him, who had consoled him
tentatively when Janie left him: came here

to be telling somebody: we had
a great funeral for him, became natives
of our own New Orleans by needing

the music we had loved for decades,
needing it to grieve publicly for Charlie,
achieved publicity: John Gleason

and Marian Holmes called me, that night,
to open their hearts, if briefly: surely that must have
meant something: yet my own wife left me

before that year was over: life goes on, Charlie,
and your friends still love you, helplessly,
no better than you loved yourself—

no, better, we wouldn't have harmed you
if we could have helped it, and you did
harm yourself graciously, with a weird dignity

through all the DTs and convulsions
and humiliations of your life and death:
Charlie, I honor you after a year in the grave

and praise myself and others, Jim, Wohler,
Carl and Sue, Mike Fay, Denis, Janie, Julie,
Valerie, all of us, because we have been your friends.

A Visit to Lonesome John: Autumn Coming

Held
    in a hollow of the hills
        the lake between

hills overgrown with pine
    jeffrey and lodgepole
        piñon over the ridge amidst

juniper, joshua
    and here
        cedar and spruce, silvertip

fir, amidst this
    varied forest, the
        lake

held back to irrigate
    citrus groves down around Redlands
        these ninety years:

Big Bear
    where Benjamin Davis Wilson
        and his brave Mexican cowboys

captured eleven grizzly bears
    twice
        the twenty-two of them

by lassos, from horseback
    when this was Hatauva
        ancestral home of the Serrano

coyote moiety:
    you lasso the bear
        to keep it from attacking

your partner,
    who lassos it
        to keep it from attacking

you:
    good timing
        from a frightened horse:

brave cowboys!
    They captured the town too
        seven women

and some children, Benjamin
    Morongo among them
        as is recorded

in Wilson's memoir
    written for Bancroft
        though he doesn't name any Indians.

All under the water now, and the old dam
    my dad saw a cow walking out on
        one dry year in the thirties

submerged too still
   though Treasure Island
      is on an isthmus now, the bay

dry
   where John Fisher's uncle
      built this cabin, back then.

We go down to the water with
   the children: Sarah, Pascal, Rufie,
      us two men

picking up beer cans and broken
   glass, pop
      tops, in a plastic bag,

to a crumbly
   decomposed granite beach
      at the edge of the lake.

The wind,
   a prevailing westerly,
      sweeping up the canyon and over

the dam,
   writes
      all knowledge on the water,

the surface of the lake:
   ripples
      coming to shore are

reflected,
    the outgoing ripples
        go under the

ripples advancing to shore:
    and they all refract
        the afternoon sunlight

so that on the yellow ground
    under the lake
        visible

through the rather clear
    water, rows of light
        advance, and are complicated

by the reflection of the
    ripples, a complication
        recomplicated

by refraction back through the
    ripples. Each point
        on the shore

becomes a source
    by these reflections
        and a passing

speed boat or cat's paw of breeze
    creates its own
        series of ripples or advancing

waves. Considered as a bounded surface
   the lake preserves
      at any moment

a point exactly where it was
   at some earlier time
      considered to be the origin

according to Brouwer's theorem
   the fixed point theorem
      so useful in deriving

for instance
   existence proofs in differential
      equations:

there is a solution
   where you can find it
      or not, or

there is no solution
   so it's okay to quit
      trying to find it:

"in essence"
   according to Sandy Grabiner
      "complicated problems

about surfaces
   become simple
      problems about groups."

The play of ripples
    water and light
        on surface and ground

could receive whatever intensity
    of attention
        one cared to give

for as long as one
    cared
        to continue.

Lonesome John is up here
    "writing his dissertation"
        so his wife can try out

how it would be to be
    separated;
        we have come up to visit him

with her and their kids.
    He'll be here
        until the pipes freeze

for winter.
    She wanted us
        so they wouldn't be

alone awake together
    and for the mountain highway
        she justly fears

driving, the way she drives.
    The wives come down to the shore.
        I give Mary a précis

of my three hours'
    observation of ripples:
        "You see, I haven't been entirely

idle"; she answers (as one who suffers from it)
    "You're always thinking
        about something."

We go back to the cabin.
    Lonesome John opines
        that observation of the

elements
    is endlessly
        fascinating:

ripples for instance
    on water,
        fire,

wind in the form of tornadoes
    or other forms of wind,
        earthquakes

what was the other?
    Wood, I said.
        Wood?

In the Far East
   there are five elements,
      water

fire and air
   metal
      and wood.

These trees
   are taller now than when
      I was a child here

my dad can see that
   though to me
      since I'm taller now myself

they look about the same.
   Climax forest coming back
      after being logged over

a hundred and some years
   ago. Fire,
      and waves on the water

or floods, but people
   he said
      are what are really

more interesting
   politically for instance
      as in his dissertation

but alone here
fire, he said,
in the fireplace

the hearth of home
or a forest fire
fire

is endlessly fascinating.
When a speedboat goes by
say a CrisCraft

with a water skier
fast enough, the ripples
arriving at the shore

are tall enough
that the crest advances
faster than

the trough
according to a formula
relating speed of wave

to a depth of water;
they crash over
like little ocean waves

making Brouwer's theorem irrelevant
which can only apply to continuous
surfaces:

brown needles among the green,
   dead jeffries
      some felled or fallen

some standing
   look sick:
      maybe the smog is doing it.

As a guest I split
   some chunks of a fallen log
      for the fireplace

with a hammer and only two
   wedges
      at the risk of getting

both of the
   wedges
      stuck, but always

in the nick of time
   the log splits
      and I get them out.

The children, ceremonious,
   know how to share a meal
      on vacation

in the mountains.
   They go to bed
      in the silent starry night

in the mountains
    we grownups
        sit by the fire

his wife
    goes to sleep on the couch
        before the conversation is over

my wife
    goes to bed beside me
        but not with me

by the dying fire
    of pine logs in the raftered
        living room of the cabin

she sleeps too.
    The children
        awaken in the basement;

I go down,
    talk to them until they sleep
        and pace

quietly the porch
    looking at the dark trees
        the far lake

the brilliant sky of the dry
    night in the mountains,
        Jupiter

and Venus
    amidst the late rising
        winter constellations.

You couldn't say it had been
    a fun summer
        welcome autumn

and the cold
    resumption of responsibilities
        activities

and their forgetfulness:
    goodbye to my own soul
        or the ravening

creature that follows me
    that caught up to me
        that night I was Jacob

the wrestler
    all night
        that other night

I can't even remember
    the many nights
        I slept and awoke in anger:

O,
    good
        night.

Stars and the pines
   and the night wind over the water
      of Big Bear Lake.

Benjamin Morongo
   died on the reservation
      down at Banning

he recorded
   the best version
      of the Serrano creation myth

among other things;
   his father, his
      uncle

were famous too in their day
   and Benjamin Davis
      Wilson became

famous and no doubt rich
   the first Anglo mayor of Los Angeles
      made innovations

in citrus culture,
   horticulture,
      his grandson was General Patton

a just man, agent
   for the Indians in his time
      when their best bet was reservations

a brave man my god
   you ought to read his story,
      deposed

for the historian Bancroft
   and now to be found
      in the Bancroft collection

at the Doe Library
   of the University
      of California.

The rest of us, Lonesome John,
   Anne, Pascal,
      Mary and me and Rufie,

Sarah and Jessica
   unsung
      til now.

A breeze falls toward the lake
   here, but somewhere
      according to Brouwer's theorem

there must be
   on the surface of the earth
      a place

where there isn't any wind at all:

somewhere
   at any given moment
      even this.

A Lake on the Earth: The Swarm

Dawn over Bicycle Lake days after a storm   a breeze fans
water on the flooded playa   and there is another movement
in it, innumerable tiny things touching the surface every-
where   as if a fine rain were still falling : ephemeral crusta-
ceans each one barely an inch long   are roiling the murky
water with gilled feet   come near the edge of it   they see
you and scoot away with amazing quickness.

What can they find to eat, some kind of algae, bacteria wet by
the same storm : here in the damp silt not the track of a bird
nor a bird hovering over the water   no coyote, rat or chuck-
walla, no creature eats them while they live   they live so
briefly and so seldom   they are brownish in color   shaped
rather like horseshoe crabs or like sperm, they are the color of
the water : as far as the eye can see their life has nothing to
do with any other.

The morning deepens, the noon sun   gives a light so white it
whitens the hills that are every color morning and evening   a
white crust round the wet edge of the water creeps inward as
the water thickens   the leaf foot twelve day race is nearing
climax   twelve days flailing the lake to get from the old egg
to the new   and when it's over, not another trace of any of
them in that flat dry lake or playa : this repeated without
variation since the Triassic.

What beguiles us is precision, how eggs by themselves can
measure rain just enough   to begin that great throb of life
that has to go all the way   and being extreme remain single,
the all including the numerous exactly   even at night they
keep up their continual motion squirming to full size in a nick
of time   taken out in a jar or tray they die in an hour : their
only element   this thin layer of water they stir between earth
and air   throughout their urgent stubborn intermittent life
in tremendous profusion.

They are not a lesson to us, the north star is not a beacon   the
moon is not luna, is not semele, is all she ever has been, the
stars   do not gleam on the water, they are not cities or
pathways   even if someone perceive and something seem
to be measured   to measure, even, to answer, rhyme, be
kosmos : it's all in the mind

Listen:
            the exhalation of water into the desert air   moistens
the shiny dark leaves of the greasewood   the pale burro
bush   the fine mud shrinks opening precise tessellations, tiles
that later crumble in the sun   a dust devil comes by like a
dervish   a thought spinning counterclockwise   dune buggies,
jeep tracks over the playa, the wind : you are here

with me, in this poem, and it
has been here for one day

FEW AND FAR BETWEEN
(1994)

Up Home Where I Come From

Roy Smith ran traps for furs
but a hawk got caught in one of them

spreading its wings, there in the trap
turning its sharp beak toward him

as he came to get it out, its glaring eyes so deep
they seemed to open onto another world in there

and steady: thus the hawk in times past
came to be an image of aristocracy.

One leg hung by a tendon; with his sharp pocketknife
Roy cut it off and left it lay

but brought the hawk home
to feed it til it got well.

There in his basement, in a hutch built for rabbits,
it glared at us with its unfathomable eyes,

accepted the dead meat he brought it, even hamburger,
unquenched. That wildness

is what we can know of dignity.
We aspire to it ourselves but seldom—

seldom. Nailed to the tree
Jesus must have been as still as that,

as wild. And I'd say
that was the right way to be, there.

Later it got well and he let it go,
our hearts leapt up when we saw it

living somehow in the wild with its one leg:
in its life we felt forgiven.

Probably it learned to pin its prey to the ground
and eat there, running that risk.

Risen, that was one thing Jesus did too:
showed he was alive and could still eat.

Every Man His Own Cross

My father wept aloud in the night. My mother
tried to comfort him, but couldn't. O,

the world would have to be intricately cruel
to make him cry like that, cruel in its need

and he alone, unable in the face of it, and don't think
there was anything he could do he hadn't tried:

you'd never find a more unsparing man than he.
"And what about the boy?" he cried out, meaning me:

I was listening dismayed in my bed. I
was a coward, and lazy, and no help, he said.

He put me on his list of failures, or of the cruel things
the world had done to him, that night. And I agreed.

Looking back now, I think he saw me in his place, unspared,
unworthy, doomed to defeat like him no matter how eagerly

and angrily, or even how patiently, and for how long a time
I would try. Like him. And he was right.

There'd be more to say, there will be, but I
would just as soon start from that. I do, still, agree.

Audacity

Joe Henk could use two powder wedges at once—black
     powder
to blast great discs sawn from a log into smaller chunks.

He'd look around and dodge what flew when the one went
     off,
finish driving the other, light it, go find the first one, hot,

fill it with powder, cut fuse, drive it, dodge, and so on—
the timing—there seems to be

an everyday audacity to life.
O, anybody's. Life.

Trolling: The Truth by Touch

"If it's a trout, you'll know it.
If you only think it is, it isn't,"
said my father: his delicate foot felt through the lake
holding the butt of his rod as he rowed,
slowly, without any splash, and just at the speed
to flop the spinners over luringly, down there:
trolling over to where we chummed up for the day.
Meat fishermen then and proud of it, or say
we wouldn't have done it just for fun. But
it was fun. Or was it? We didn't have to know
if it was any fun or not. Or cold,
or boring all day keeping the boat dead silent—
still fishing and I do mean still—
and the day it snowed, in the middle of May,
it was hard to numb salmon eggs onto the hook
but the fish were really biting, that day. Myself—

well—not knowing for sure once I towed a trout
clear over from Orchard Bay to Movie Point.
All his frantic struggle to escape that pain in the mouth
could have been just the line tugging at lakeweed
time after time. He felt like a weed clump when I reeled in
the sluggish weight of him, gill flattened, drowned maybe,
and I was wrong again (but I had the fish)

and in spite of being that kind of son,
with that kind of father, I know:
some things you only think are so, are so.

Clearing the Way

You could say it was work he did for wages
sixty hours without rest when my father
as a young man set out after a storm
to clear the road from Burnt Mill to Fawnskin
in the big new rotary plow, the SnoGo.
That was back half a century now,
a hundred and ninety horsepower engine
doesn't seem so big but it was then:
a Climax Machine, straight six,
and each piston the size of your head.
Compared to what we have today
the whole machine would seem ungainly
and small; and it took more from the men.
He had a swamper, who didn't drive
but wiped the windshield by hand, got out
in the storm to help fit new shear pins
when they broke, and greased his share
of the hundred and sixty points they had to grease
every time they came to a station; there
they'd eat something, too, because
they didn't carry food in the cab. Work!
My dad bundled close to the windshield to see
through a small hole he cleared from the inside
and at night they had what seemed strong lights
to pick out the orange poles sticking up
so as to mark where the road was, under drifts
along Shovel Hill and past Heaps Peak.
The backscratcher clawed down the snow,

the augurs moved it into a fan, that blew
it up in the air, a great plume of white
that fell somewhere far from the road;
they roared on eastward along the Rim of the World.
Then the blizzard came on again, and filled in
the road behind them with winddriven, drifted snow.
See the great blizzard sweeping over the mountains,
snow falling slantwise or nearly level, and somewhere in it
that other little jet of snow blown upward like a spout
as they kept on ahead clearing the part of the road where
    they were.
Was it work then? Because a road like that
will be covered with snow again some time
no matter how well you clear it, or else
melt clear by itself if you wait for summer;
that's all the work we have, in a little area
we can influence between what won't happen,
ever, and what would surely happen anyway.
They plowed straight through Running Springs,
serviced the truck at Dry Creek, and kept on
past Deer Lick Meadows, the Emerald Inn
where McGlinchy gave them some Irish whiskey
(snowed in there with his pet coon, Oscar),
on past Arrowbear and the Green Valley turnoff,
day and night; Snow Valley and Lake View Point
where they serviced again and went on around
the Arctic Circle, down to the dam at Big Bear
and then along the north shore of the lake
to Fawnskin where they filled up with gasoline
carried over from Pine Knot, three drums
by dog sled across the ice, and then,

since the road had closed in behind them,
they headed back. Sixty hours of that,
the blizzard gave out before they did, that time.
They just kept on plowing in the dark and the sunshine
until when they got to Running Springs
they found the road open ahead of them,
people out playing in the snow, making snowmen,
somebody towing a skier behind a pickup.
They decided to knock off work then, and rest.

Being Up There During the World War

When the attack bomber hit Keller Peak in the storm
it was my dad and his crew that took toboggans up to it
in the snow, on what he called a one-to-one slope (45
    degrees):
that may not sound so steep, but when you're there it is.

Ira Vincent got sick, the bodies were so scattered.
The men gathered the parts at a guess which went with
    which
except for the bombardier, folded over the Norden bomb-
    sight.
They took it down still wrapped that way, it was so secret.

The deputy sheriffs kept warm in the hut by the ski lift
halfway across the mountain from where the plane hit.
They were the ones the paper said went up for the bodies.
Well, they did come up to our world from the valley where
    they lived.

We read that story, and other things the paper said had
    happened
the same way as usual. It didn't mention granite.

Learning Death

for Bert Meyers

You take a rattlesnake or a bat, they're
quick. I knew a boy who thought
he was a terrific shot when he'd hit one
but I think they'd go after the bullet and hit it.

Nights outside his cabin in the pine quiet dark
with a flashlight beam to bring the bats
or the bugs the bats were after: that summer
the gnats and mosquitos got fierce

and the time beside the trail backed up to rocks
I thought I saw the snake strike:
trying to protect himself that way, without any
legs or arms: then had no head either.

I remember a cracker looking at
one of Ray Folsom's blacksnakes:
he told his son, "They're poisonous, I know,
I killed hundreds of them back home"

but I'd say the cracker was the poisonous one,
if that was the way he had to find out:
poisonous in his mind. He saw a killer
but didn't know it was him

and while it's true that bats have rabies sometimes
I never saw one tangled in anyone's hair
nor had any trouble at all with bats:
thousands of them flying past my face when I went in a
        cave.

That boy, who thought he had the skill
to keep rabies away, to keep all snakebite from happening,
to keep death far away—he went on and made money
but it didn't help him: he fended off his life

and he still doesn't know how death is
like food flying, or like bad news, and how sometimes
the quick and the brave are the first to get it
while the rest of us, skillful or wary or slow,

take our share of it with us wherever we go
until one day, swerving or lunging the best we can
we'll catch up with something twisting along hot and
        straight
before we know, and that'll be it.

No fear, no blame any more, just it: as if

a rope of dust twisted a certain way
traveled on end for miles over the hills one day
then came untwisted, frayed finally into a breeze
from the west, and settled down over another part of the
        desert.

Dusk Was Falling

As dusk was falling I came to a cabin:
yellow lamplight fell from its windows
onto the bluewhite snow, and inside
were hospitable people, a man and wife
who invited me "Come in and get warm."
Fire in a woodstove, a kerosene lamp,
shelves of books, that cabin odor—
O, and coffee left over, that I took
in a rustic comfortable rocking chair,
hardwood branches bent to shape
with the bark still on them, and shellacked.
They were on vacation, but as we talked
they let me feel what weight life had
for them, and they felt mine.
Their son had disappeared, they didn't know why;
he started home from college in his car
and was never heard from. It was the Lord's way,
they thought, but couldn't understand. Would I pray
for them, and for their son? I said
I'd pray the best I could for us all,
and lingered there for a while, cherished
in their cabin, a son to their need,
while outside night came on and it got colder.
I had my own journey to go, and it
wasn't getting any shorter;
I believe I stayed about long enough,
so they were glad to see me go
and the cabin warmth hadn't got in me

so deep a few quick shivers
wouldn't shake it away, in the cold.
There wasn't a moon, but the stars were close
and the snow gave back their light;
I could see my breath in the still air,
like a little friend, that I'd leave behind,
again, and again, and again.

Example and Admonition

My father's admonition: when given
a choice, choose the path that
leads uphill, always,

so up we went, but all led down soon after:
our destination Deep Creek, where water had gathered
by taking every downhill opportunity.

We thought of that when the higher path turned down,
but no one mentioned it then, nor ever, in fact, til now.
Two lessons: and though sometimes I feel clever,

and have read the Chou I book all about that water,
I've not forsaken either one. If there be something in a man
that flows uphill, he has to go with it

whatever sweat or humiliation may attend his going.
Done patiently, this is called "matching heaven with heaven."
Otherwise, just strife.

Few and Far Between

If only we could forgive ourselves, and didn't
have to have somebody else forgive us—

Where I came from everybody could see anyone coming,
even storms: and out there the etiquette

was not to say right off what you came for when you did
or ask anybody why, if they came where you were

in all space, and time; it made for a kind
of trust, or—well, it was like trust.

I remember some of those storms, how the dust
would kick up before them in the wild wind, and behind it

the blueblack cloud piled high white on top
with lightning flaring inside, and maybe only a few miles
        wide,

coming over the desert sort of slow and grand:
you could have got out of the way if you wanted to

but nobody did; as I said, seldom enough is welcome.
Didn't I say that? One night when mother was away

my dad and I followed a storm clear down
to Needles in the state car. His job

was to take care of the highway, so it was work, sort of,
for us to ride along behind that cloud we could see by its
    own light

through the wild fragrance the desert has after a rain
in the lone car on the road that night, to keep track

of the damage it did. He showed me a place near Essex
where a flash flood had ripped out three hundred feet of
    roadbed

two years before, where it hadn't rained
in fifty years before that. The foreman said so,

Billy Nielson, and he'd been there fifty years
without seeing the ground wet.

My dad and I stopped on the grade below Goffs
and watched the storm go on out of his territory

across the river into Arizona
where the sky was getting gray,

and turned for home as the sun rose behind us
back across the clean desert in slant light

that lit the smoke trees in washes that were churned
    smooth
where the water went, and sharpened along the edges

through Essex and Cadiz Summit, great tamarisked
     Chambless,
Ludlow for breakfast with the humorous Chinaman, Lee,

Newberry Springs, Daggett and Elephant Butte, Nebo
     hidden by wire,
on home over the hill to Barstow on the good road.

Willie Boy

If you were a young Paiute in 1905, and got arrested
for drunken disturbance of the Anglo peace
and the sheriff took your picture in the county jail,
you'd look okay—you'd look about the way Willie Boy did,
inward during adversity, solitary, brave enough;
but if I were a young Paiute in 1909, and wished somehow
to alleviate solitude, and tried to become intelligible,
got a white shirt with sleeve garters, a necktie
with polkadots, a pretty good hat, and even a fountain pen,
then went to a photographer in Banning and paid him
to take my picture, I'd have that blank mad hopeless look,
an expression you see now and then on an outlaw horse,
fierce but drawn back, my eyes the wrong side out.
It's the look of a man who knows nobody sees things his way,
whatever wavering way that might be—knows, and can't say.
Come down the dry side of the mountain, you get into
        juniper and piñon pine
then at a certain elevation you see a lone greasewood or
        Joshua
among the granite boulders—what is there to say about that.
Maybe it was a woman made him feel that way—not that
        she willed it
but it was his reaction. Let him go, then, let him kill to get her
then kill her too when she can't keep pace in flight over the
        desert;
hounded down let him shoot three horses from under the
        posse

54

but hit one of the men, a white man, in dismay—
that won't make him intelligible. Back in town
the reporters interpreted him to their own community,
"the Beau Brummel of the Indian colony," a suitor
"whose ardor fanned by opposition always disappeared
when conquest was complete"—smug ignorance
to which everything is equally falsely intelligible—
when the blowflies had beat them to it and got it right.
Let the fire have the last word, smoke, stink and light.
Let the metal parts of his suspenders mark the place
fifty years with their name, SHIPLEY or is it SHIRLEY
    PRESIDENT.
Let the granite boulders keep quiet, as if it didn't make any
    difference.

Helendale: Waiting by the Mojave River

Beeeeeeeeeeeeeeeeeeeeeeeeeeeeee:

A night wreck out on the highway
left one driver crushed unconscious against the horn,

so: an alfalfa farmer got up
and set fire to his barn, as a beacon, for angels.

He'd been listening, as he lay there, for Gabriel,
and thought that horn was his trumpet blowing the Second
    Coming

all the rest of that night.
Toward morning the barn went out.

Crews came and carried off the wrecked cars,
the hurt and the done for; at sunup

there was only the black smudge of rubber
on the red pavement, charred beams of the barn,

the hulk of a tractor he'd left parked
inside. Red eyed with spent feelings, that farmer,

being up already, went on about his business:
he worked on a fence, and let in the irrigation

still listening just the same. And his one mistake—
or I'd have to say his other mistake—was

he told the insurance agent how it happened,
was laughed at, got angry, had to quit

the Kiwanis Club after a fight, and he felt lonely
until he thought: "Well:

I reckon if Noah could take it, so can I."

Bees in the Blossoms

An early bee amid eucalyptus blossoms
took on more nectar than she could carry:

not that it was so heavy, but so cold. Down
fell the bee, where others had fallen,

strewn plentifully over the dirt like petals
or like seeds. A breakfasting horny toad

wears a garland of stingers inside her lip,
she doesn't seem to mind. See how the bees

buzz their wings, to get warm, how they
clean themselves, all over, unload their nectar,

buzz again, to fly, no use, until
sunlight begins to warm them and some do fly.

Alluvium: A Reply

Somewhere two rivers rush together at the foot of a scarp,
meander over a coastal plateau, then down a barranca

the rio caudal plunges into its deep estuary
and huge canyons under the sea. But here

on this nearly level delta wide as the eye can see
streams mingle and separate, some sweet, some brack

some sink under their own silt, are lost in the arrowweed
where a curve of current earlier carved the bank

some dwindle down sloughs under poplar or willow,
the heron's home, some into quicksand, and

nothing is turning out the way you thought it would be,
nothing.

September, 1950

A dance in the dorm at Scripps College
and none of us had Shinola.
Undauntedly, Stone
instead used brilliantine.

We stepped forth to the fandango
over mown lawns of CMC
in the long twilight of late summer.
Grass halms clung to his feet.

Our troops were in retreat
on the outskirts of Pusan;
the tide was rising, rising,
that would propel us to Inchon.

Rich girls in peasant blouses,
the music, the flowers in their hair!
How little we understood, and we knew it
when that awkward, ugly decade began.

Goodbye Big Ed

Little he thought when he hid out in his own house
for the pleasure of stomping burglars enticed by the dark
that he'd die, and die young, and in great pain like this,
thrown from his bike at speed where he broke his neck

and lay five hours on boulders in the creekbed
until death took him at last. Little he thought
about any of it: the preacher was right when he said
Big Ed wasn't afraid to die. Whenever he fought

it was for fun, or a good turn, or sheer pride of life.
See him armed in his undershirt, out in his back yard
the new boulevard had cut through, by the clothesline,
hollering I'LL GIVE YOU SOMETHING TO STARE AT,
        FAGGOT

down to someone stopped at the traffic light, meaning
no harm by it, really: not meaning anything.

Bill Munsen, An Elegy

He came sauntering along the street where my truck was
at midnight, as if just happening by:

he'd been waiting for hours in the bushes,
it was obvious, said he wanted a ride

to the Rancherita so we gave it to him, but there
he wouldn't get out, begged us to take him on

to Tijuana where he knew we three were going,
leave him at the Long Bar he said.

McClain jerked him out the back of the truck,
slammed him into the cab, and said "Let's go"—

Munsen there defiant on the curb, "You think you're
so fuckin smart"—Kirby lost all respect for him then,

when he didn't fight. We went along
that night, played crazy liars' dice in a café,

had a good time though McClain came down on me
for my stories in Quixote magazine

because of their sentimentality: a scene
fraught with intensity. I played him chess for my life

but won. Kirby was shaken too,
McClain was both our guru back then.

When I left him off next morning in La Jolla
Mac said "Maybe I'll never see you again."

Munsen killed himself soon after, drove over
the median divider and went out in a headon

which we thought was a chickenshit way to do it,
inconsiderate as always—though the other driver

only had his legs broken, which didn't bother him
much—he was a tough tuna boat captain

Mac went to see in the hospital.
Naturally, he was pissed off.

The Mojave in March

The desert at this season
        disfigured by green
                what life there is thriving

as it can
        tiny white poppies, these
                ephemeral grasses, filaree:

to me
        it looks cleaner
                when it's brown

the rest of the year
        rock colored land
                in shifting light

and shadow.
        As for me
                I need a shave,

need not thrive
        I mean
                need not to

this penitential season.

Another Part of the Desert

When his fire went out the stars came closer:
he had more company then but it was colder:

little stars, or far, he hadn't seen in years,
scales of the Dragon, ribs of the Bear, the Lion's whiskers:

those elegant constellations! And he like a rush of sparks
flying upward from a log kicked in a campfire

belonged in the midst of them while they all
went their separate ways and flared out or winked out,

he thought; still, it was cold, he couldn't stay there, he got up
and went on by the light of his old friends

slapping his sides like a cock to keep warm
and chanting a song to the rhythm of it, how the ocean

wouldn't make him a beakful of water: Mexican macho
    cock:
and that felt like a lie, but it cheered him up.

Whenever he stumbled, he said "Excuse me" to the rock
but thought that maybe that dislodging was the right step

in a dance so intricate he'd never catch on to the beat,—
not knowing that all the while his own ribs and whiskers

were guiding stars to multitudes, lit
calamitously or serenely by their own light.

A Word Like Fire

The prophet that hath a dream, let him tell a dream
Jeremiah, ch. xxiii

In my sickness I withered from one shape
to another: finally I was a little dry spider.

The doctor put me down somehow into two holes
in the wet sand, and went away. I was to wait there

until I got well or died, when the sand dried
and caved in on me; that would be time for my resurrection

in this life or the other. What is the chaff to the wheat?
saith the Lord, Is not my word like a fire?

saith the Lord, and like a hammer
that breaketh the rock into pieces?

Jeremiah wept to say it, but I find
I still have some eagerness for this experience:

the doctor goes away but the Lord
goes down with each of us into the grave.

That was my dream, and I am afraid
but have taken a dare from Holy Writ to say it

and may the name of the Lord, or his billion names,
be praised, I shall praise them for ever and ever.

I knew what it said, only it seemed incredible,
not anything you'd want to say out loud

in the world, that has its own enervating problems
with their own ineffective solutions, its detestable hopes

that are like hopes I have myself or have had
(they come away like the nail from the quick);

is that what it's like to be naked: nailless, eyeless,
given to visions, aflame: and what a cool breeze then

flows like neutrinos through your empty spaces.
I have felt it like clouds of them billowing through.

This World

That sudden movement will attract
a child to any insect—which (if it
succeed in catching it) it
will crush out: that very thing

unless the child have a wise father
who can fashion a tiny halter of thread
so then the greeny gold beetle will fly and fly
and the child keep it as a toy.

Another September

On the gimbals of the equinox everything is about to turn,
is turning: pyracantha berries neither green nor red,
the yellow poplar still mainly green, the green
of the gingko dimmed, that will change to bright yellow
quick as a traffic light, sycamore, ash, persimmon, peach,
summercanopied yet but with fringes fallen at their feet,
the crepe-myrtle glorious in bloom, the naked ladies—
when into this falls a fetid rain, chilled here to fall,
and snow on the high peaks, but a summer storm
out of the Gulf—the kind of thing we didn't have for thirty
    years
but have again now something else is turning.
The odor of it rises from the sidewalk. The light
under raincloud brings all colors to vivid life.

Sturnus Vulgaris

A starling shits as it flies, alights
on a power wire over the street:

spies a loquat in the gutter and
flutters down in a hurry;

that's a starling, always busy.
Meanwhile up high somewhere

a mockingbird has been singing
and singing, that elegant predator;

now it comes paratroopering down
still chirping in air, alights

with a flourish that drives the starling away,
struts around the loquat cocking its long tail:

while the starling, short tailed, hunched in flight,
aims its yellow beak with starling purposefulness

somewhere else, flying straight as if it
wished it were a bullet. And that's not all.

Things like this keep happening all the time.

On a Painting by David Hockney

Why doesn't she object to him
revealing her that pitilessly, her
swimming pool living room
the exact slump of her shoulder
the expensive droop of her sundress
her worn anxious elegant face?
Her stuffed antelope head that looks just like her?
And he such a famous painter
all her friends would see it and
know it. "Exactly. There it is
exactly, my cunt of a life."
In case you thought it was so easy being
a Beverly Hills housewife.

Thin Ice

The father has come to Scripps Pool
to be with his wife and children.

Not to swim: he is in his slacks and penny
loafers; but they all came together in her car,

the blue Datsun. The girls are excited,
one almost two, one three: they bring him dead leaves

from a magnolia. "Did you ever see
such a big leaf?" he asks. "Are you ready

to crackle it?" They do this repeatedly. He crackles the
     leaves.
The girls remain excited, increasing in wonder

as their game goes on and on. Again
and again they cause him to exclaim

and to crackle the leaves. Having begun it
falsely, he doesn't know how to bring it

to an end. The wife, for whom he is doing all of it,
looks on. She can't stop it either.

Shoot Out

Niels Bohr noticed in Westerns that at the draw
the first man to go for his gun was always killed.
The other, who waited for that, was quicker.

Was it because the first man had to decide to shoot,
while the other, just reacting, could take a short cut?
That's what Bohr thought.

When I'd have explained by the plot: the bad guy wins
toward the middle, the good guy has to wait his turn.
That's how you know the bad guy. He knows it too,

and gloats for awhile, then loses his nerve
when he gets hints the movie is about to end.
According to the script. The scriptures. Amen.

But what if Bohr was right? And what if the script
is lost, or not even lost, but just forgotten?
And what if the wind hones the edge of my house?

I'm comin to get you, Tex.

Con los Hombres a Robar, con los Cabrones ni al Agua

She came in naked, for her glasses,
trying not to interrupt this. "I can't help it," she said.

No need to look behind things for a theory.
The "blue" "sky" for instance: that's a theory.

The wounded jay turned toward me, defiant,
threatening with its little black beak.

It was an advantage, coming ahead like that.
Had it been the other way, that would have been the
     advantage.

No, it isn't any help. Wisdom is wisdom,
help is help. Didn't you know that?

Bagdad Chase Road in July

Within the immense circle of the horizon
only the two of us on two legs
that don't have feathers on. Hello,
horned lark. Hello, loggerhead shrike.
Hello, dove-size bird with black fan-tail
fluttering along the ground, a jackrabbit
would jump as high. And for the vast
absence of our own species,
thanks, thanks, thanks. Not that you
didn't dig the mines and make this road
we're on; but it's your absence
today that earns my gratitude. Thanks too
for the monument and bronze tablet
to mark where Ragtown was, and the railroad
going down to Ludlow, so I can rejoice
they've already all disappeared
with hardly a trace. Thank you sky
for speaking only after lightning. Hello, jackrabbit,
hello groundsquirrel, good luck raven,
I never saw you hover like that.
Thank you, rain, for flavoring our jaunt
with a hint of danger, and for the splashy mist
when you lashed the desert hills to show
what you can do when you mean business.
Thank you, other twolegged bare featherless creature,
for sharing the jagged horizon of my life.
Thank you rainbow over the East Mojave
low to the ground so early in the afternoon:
thank you for being here with us.

GRANITE INTRUSIVE

Granite Intrusive

Where the clean wind scours the rock—
sun like a hammer, ice the other season—
there's the life, said the lichen,
that's the life for me.

I'm so glad we found this place
murmured the moss
before the tourists came.

Root of a palo blanco
in thin bark like white paper
crept down over bare rock
to annex another spoonful of soil
and murder the moss that had made it:
I like a place that's been spoiled
just enough, said the root, snuggling in.

The rock didn't say anything at all.
Why would it?

The Silver Dollar in Boron

It might have been a beer bar anyplace
but it wasn't—it was on the Mojave desert
not far from Edwards air force base.

A juke box, pool tables, dim reddish light,
stories of lives that had started out somewhere else—
then the door would open and everything turn white

as a blast of desert sunlight would come in
with another stranger, who would grope toward a barstool
when the door closed and the room got dim again

while we sheltered there from that sharp horizon,
that strafing light, and the wind.

Omega over the North Mojave

Those jet fighters dove for the town, passed out of sight
they went so near the ground, later arched up, three of them,
jetting white vapor to write the letter great O like a judgment
over Ridgecrest and China Lake. We had our picnic lunch
in a little park, shaded by the bushy sapling of an exotic
    pine.

Across the way two firemen, up on the rack
where they dry hoses after a fire, watched through binoculars
that fierce, precise, expensive play, while ravens
behaved the way they would on any other Sunday.
Out of all that might have happened, not much did

yet even what did was infinite. And the planes
swung round for another flyover, snapping in the air—
one rocked like a recliner chair before it leveled out
and went on in.

To a Horn in York Minster

carved in Salerno, 11th century
given to the Minster by Ulf before the Norman
Conquest

The wealthy man, today the dust of earth,
Survives in this rare gift. His name was Ulf.
Italian craftsmen carved an elephant tusk
Which he gave, at last vainly, against death.

Death is equally vain. The Norman came
And swept away or pauperized Ulf's race,
Driven in turn by epic destinies;
This horn is now his symbol and his name.

In spite of the long death or slavery
The lordly hand confers this ivory.
The donor's shade is present here. I feel

I am myself a shade in shadow—a moment,
And the moment is but ash, not diamond.
And only what is past is true or real.

after Borges

Trophy Hunt (for the Way Things Used to Be)

These are the sheep with curly horns
that roam the wild Mojave.

These are the wardens duly sworn
who guard the sheep with curly horns
as they roam the wild Mojave.

These are the hunters who drew the numbers
for a license at fifty thousand dollars
to pay the wardens duly sworn
and harvest some rams with curly horns
out on the wild Mojave.

These are protectors of animal rights
who came out and camped in the dark of night
to spook the rams and spoil the plans
of the lucky hunters who drew the numbers
and paid the wardens duly sworn
for a shot at a ram with curly horns
out on the wild Mojave.

These are the sheriff's deputies
called by the hunters to keep the peace
and prevent the protectors of animal rights
from chasing sheep in the dark of night
to save the rams and spoil the plans
of the lucky hunters who drew the numbers
and paid the wardens duly sworn

for some trophy rams with curly horns
out on the wild Mojave.

These are the Channel Seven reporters
with their camera crews and helicopters
who followed the sheriff's deputies
called by the hunters to keep the peace
and prevent the protectors of animal rights
from chasing sheep in the dark of night
to save the rams and spoil the plans
of the lucky hunters who drew the numbers
and paid the wardens duly sworn
to kill a few rams with curly horns
out on the wild Mojave.

And this is me in my living room
with the light turned off and the TV on
and I wonder what happened to all of us
that left us in such an awful mess
with our helicopters and television
and our ball parks that have to be air conditioned,
yearning for days when we shot our food
and life was hard and hungry and good:
days you'd seldom see anyone
out there on the wild Mojave.

Santana

Weather off the desert, the air so clear
it makes night darker here in the city.

Seventh Street I come along on my bicycle
is a black river or abyss for all I can see.

Whatever light there is
just goes on wherever it's going and doesn't come back.

Many a star shines into this black valley
between camphor trees that are barely visible

yet I believe the pavement must be there.
Under my wheel I can hear it go clack clack clack.

Alligator cracks. Tameless night. If I didn't believe
this would be floating, or flight.

Erles

Half crushed at the edge of a dirt track
amidst coarse crumbs of decomposed granite
lies a scorpion.
Her little ones have got down off her back.

The sun declines: shade
saves her, the lacy shadow
of a creosote bush reaches over.
She'll have to move in the morning or die.

Night and the cold: ants go back in. And then
the chitinous plates that cover her back
wither, shrink, and come apart
light passes through them

down inside her there is a vast pool of light
her flesh cracks open
the new flesh underneath feels its own coolness
it is so new, and it shines

Planets and constellations seem to wheel overhead
as the earth turning turns her face everywhere
in the heavens: Azrael, Uriel, Zadkiel wheel
in the distance: Gabriel close by:
late rising Annael, Michael hidden in the bosom of Raphael
appear in the east: the night has passed

and no beast has discovered this crippled scorpion
no coyote coati or fierce grasshopper mouse

morning is near and kestrels

she is still there
she is living

Adam Cast Forth

Was there a Garden, or was it just a dream?
Dull, in a flickering light, I've often wondered
(And almost as if it were somehow a comfort)
If the past, once Adam's kingdom, now his shame,

Couldn't have been some trick, an illusion caused
By a certain God I dreamt. The memory
Of his clear Paradise is by now blurry,
But I am sure it did exist, and does,

Though not for me. This tedious long furrow
Is my chastisement, and the incestuous war
Of all the Cains and Abels and their fry.

And still, it is a great thing to have loved,
To have been blest or lucky, to have lived
In the green Garden, if only for a day.

after Borges

Song: Mojave Narrows

To say that death is a river
and my love for you a star reflected in the river

that the river has worn a channel through boulders, and
    flows
north and east from The Forks a hundred miles without
    tributaries

to say a dry lake is a mirror, where the river
gives itself up to the sky

A Story in Blue

The coed was in the courtyard
by the jacaranda tree.

A scrub jay came to the feeder.
With its little sharp black beak

it flung spray after spray of birdseed
to one side and the other.

The tiny house with its walls of glass
was empty, quite empty.

The jay with a loud cry flew away
and she said, sotto voce,

reminds me of you you prick.

Pomona Laundresses

Gritty overalls, greasy aprons, greasy, gritty rags—
those laundresses were making the world a better place.

On their way home, a happy hour: seven stools and a
    booth
the juke box playing Pretty Woman at Vance's Place.

She had love on her mind she said and no one at home to
    do it
she said it out loud and she wasn't about to say Please.

God made us like himself: this world is like a fair
with booths and rides that fade away like flowers fair.

Her friend said Look out You'll get arrested
You're disturbing the peace, and she said What peace.

A Child Who Is Not Likable

A child who is not likable, quite lacks
the innocent coquetries of her age and sex,

knocks things over often, demands what she can get,
does not expect to be liked, and is not likable—yet

seldom frets, and never without calculation, sees
right through the phony kindness of adults she knows,

plays soberly upon their vanities, never pleads for mercy
nor for the love she isn't going to get, gets

what she has, and keeps it.

An Old Story

He started out as Prince Charming,
roused her from thunder, I mean slumber

she walked the streets of a university town
thinking "Now there's nothing I don't know"

but when the time came she was able
to change him into a dog, or was it a frog—

run it backward, withdraw the kiss, the diver
rises feet first out of the turbulence

that converges all at once and is quiet again
as with incredible precision he turns right side up

and lands on the diving board—a dog, it was a god
damn dog whose high inaudible whine can etch glass.

Like Sir Bertilak, he forgot that part
of the story, remained enchanted,

sent back the pilgrim through the wilderness
almost the way he came, call it a regress

-ion, a resumption, of his unspeakable burden,
he goes back to his wife, cries out,

reads in a book, puts it down, comes to a frantic
conclusion this was all a delusion,

and now it's starting over, everything sweeping along
like the first time but now it's not the first time,

there must be a way to crawl over the edge
of it, see it thin as it is sideways, look under,

withdraw one's own kiss, let her resume her
thunder, her slumber, the piss rise miraculously

into Xantippe's pot which she then turns over
and having caught it, holds it—holds it.

To a Dime

Windy and cold the night when I set sail
from New York City. As we cleared the harbor,
I flung from the top deck
a dime that flashed and was drowned in the black water,
a bit of light snatched away by time and darkness.
I had the sensation I had done something irrevocable,
that I had augmented the history of our planet
by two continuous, parallel, maybe infinite series:
my own destiny, made of uneasiness, and love, and vain
        vicissitude,
and that of this silvery disk
the waters were taking to soft depths
or to far seas that tumble yet
the spoils of the Viking or the Spaniard.
For each of my waking or my sleeping moments
a corresponding one belongs to that blind coin.
At times I have felt remorse
and at others envy
because like us you live in time and its labyrinth
and you don't know it.

after Borges

Bare House Blues

Don't the moon look lonesome shining through the trees

Hide-and-go-seek. "Try and find us, Daddy." Obediently
he hides his eyes. When he opens them the house
is empty. Bleak at heart he seeks them: in the pantry,

In the broom closet, behind the dining room door,
behind the armchair their mother didn't take away with her;
mirthful when found, they jump out and want to play more.

Dismayed by a husband's grief, by a father's blank terror,
he does it again: he hides his dry eyes, counts,
and then goes again to find them when they disappear.

Rain

Evening, a sudden clearing of the mist,
For now a fine, soft rain is freshening.
It falls and it did fall. Rain is a thing
That no doubt always happens in the past.

Hearing it fall, the senses will be led
Back to a blessed time that first disclosed
To the child a flower that was called *the rose*
And an extraordinary color, *red*.

These drops that blind our panes to the world outside
Will brighten the black grapes on a certain trellis
Out in the far, lost suburbs of the town

Where a courtyard was. The rain coming down
Brings back the voice, the longed-for voice,
Of my father, who has come home, who has not died.

after Borges

Age and Vigilance

George Morgan decided that Coco was vicious,
our fat eager labrador that wouldn't have meant any trouble,
but he hollered and shook his stick, was afraid and suspicious
until one day she took the hint, went over and bit his poodle.

O didn't he holler then, and when Pat went over hollered
    at her,
called the cops, and the vet, and the pound, everyone he
    could think of
until I got a bit steamed myself and called him a motherfucker,
wishing him nearer my age, I'd go knock his block off—

a goodnatured, neighborly, peaceloving man like me.
And water wells up in the ground, it burst through his
    front yard,
strange cars sometimes park unexplained on the street,
a family of jews has moved into the neighborhood,

another neighbor picks dead leaves off his ivy at night.
Something ails George's wife, the doctors can't tell him what.

Family Group Snapshot

"I don't be*lieve* this!" cries Sarah: at ten
she's already entering a season of outrage.
Ellen is nine, looks on with interest
but like someone who hears it rain
and doesn't get wet. Rufie is nine too,
a desperado in his own eyes:
he even played hooky from school
and was impenitent. Paul is eleven,
and he is interested in a girl but that's
a deep dark secret between him and his mother—
thoughts of Reason and Justice don't yet afflict him
the way they do Sarah. Louie is seven,
the cow's tail usually—hardly anyone notices
how smart he is, but he notices.

The Burial of the Dead

The Little League shortstop's dad in the stands:
tennis wives come with their husbands but cluster round him
he's so lean, and tan, and divorced, and cool, and
handsome until you get to his eyes: lights out:
a lume spento as the poet said. Don't they see that?
Or do they, and is that what they like about him?
My God, if they do what lives we're living, what lives,
and what cause for hope can any of us have
but You, when You are justly
disgusted and angry with all of us?

Chrysanthemums

The wine is poured when the cup is empty.
And everything is quiet as the sun sets;
Flocking toward the woods, birds are chirping;
Under the east balcony I shout boisterously . . .
                                    —T'ao Ch'ien (372–427)

These are the children here this afternoon
since Paul and his Rwandan friend Leslie went off to
        baseball:
Rufie and Louie, our kids, Jonah from across the street
and his little sister Is, who afternoons with us
because their mother has left home to look for herself;
Rebecca Grabiner from two doors down; Sarah
and Ellen, our kids, and Ellen's guests
Ala and Gabby: they troop after her into the kitchen
for a drink of water, abubble in the wake of her excitement.
Ellen is the hostess among us and Sarah, at nine,
just now the oldest, benignly in charge.
The boys run out of the house in sheer exuberance!
From my hammock on the porch I caution them,
Don't run in the house, and Don't go into the street
without looking; then I return to my book,
Thomas Hoccleve's *Regimen of Princes*. It's work,
sort of, for me to lie here reading this. Jonah
and Rufie get in a fight and Jonah cries: my wife
Pat tells Rufie that Jonah may be upset because
he doesn't know which parent he'll stay with tonight;
Rufie retorts "I'm not going for it!" but he goes for it.

Another swirl and all of a sudden they're a band,
or a parade: three whistles (recorders in fact
but the girls haven't the art), an autoharp,
one real drum, and the boys on biscuit tins:
a festive racket like bacchantes or a noise of waits,
and it Is a parade, down the street and back, and then
around the block. The beggar tells Hoccleve
This lyf, my sone, is but a chirie faire
that passeth soon (as Chaucer said) *as floweres faire.*
Me here in this hammock, T'ao Ch'ien drunk
on his own porch while birds fly up to roost,
my old pal Mac McCloud over in his lofty canyon
not charioted by Bacchus and his pards nor giving,
as he never has, "a rat's ass" . . . T'ao Ch'ien:
satisfied now that my humble life can go on.

My Neighbors

The silly linnet who lives next door
sings on her nest so anyone can find it:
up under the roof of the front porch,
her long unrepetitious cadenzas
break my heart. I would protect her
yet she sets up there each spring
while the other tenants arrive and leave,
arrive and leave, young in their life:
one to Japan on a fellowship, and one
to a commune in the Santa Cruz mountains
hoping to get his head together;
one to San Diego in panic, and one
to a bitter rendezvous somewhere,
I don't know where: Native American
businessman; and she sings, she sings,
she broods on her nest after the equinox
and sings "her heart out" as we'd say
and after that abundantly keeps on.

Elegy on a Spider

Well she's gone now and I'm sorry—
  the spider whose web was stretched
in the cove between wall and cupboard
  over the sink in our kitchen.

My left hand would blunder through it
  whenever I worked the light switch;
as soon as I'd gone away
  she would repair the damage

For what must have been more than a year—
  how long does a spider live?
Immortal as any bird
  she seemed not born for death

While many a victim's or husband's
  exoskeleton was left
nearly intact but empty
  hanging there in her web.

They say it was Minerva
  made Arachne into her;
my own wise wife it was
  who did away with that spider

Or only the web, the web—
  she scoured the cupboard clean
and when that job was over
  both web and spider were gone.

O only a tiny loss—
  to mourn it would be silly
but she was beautiful
  and if not a friend, familiar.

Be With Me, Beauty

We're always the same age inside, but
that forty-year-old waitress in the song
sure looks a lot better than she used to—

Can Verdier be right? Right now we don't think
we'd want to go on the way his mother is
our world a dim twilight day and night, the bedsheet

stretching out before us forever like Bonaparte's retreat,
a sore where the catheter rubs, the nurses
and everyone else tired of us and our needs,

but he says the old rarely are suicides;
you can't tell from here how it looks to her.
And he's probably right. If we ever get there

we may want more of it too, even that.
As if when all is said and done there *were*
something amazing about just being alive.

A Habitat Group

Dave's Shoe Repair was dusty;
  dust lay on counter and cases
and on faded cardboard displays
  of saddle soap, wax, heels, half soles, and laces.

I came in for a last pair of heel taps
  and a last conversation in Spanish
before the next improvement
  should cause Dave and his gluepots to vanish.

The Some Crust Bakery, adjacent,
  was expanding into a tea room.
Young Doctor Ilsley came in
  and the three of us made a quorum.

(John Ilsley was nearing retirement
  but to me he was still the Young Doctor
because I used to be treated
  by J. Morrill Ilsley, his father.)

We spoke of times we remembered
  an era long gone by
when the money came from orange groves,
  Mount Baldy was "only that high,"

And something may have been simpler,
  if subtler, in people's ways,
and the shoe repair business was steadier
  in those less affluent days:

A quiet commemoration
  that got to be like a party.
In the back room a radio was playing
  a novelty song from the forties.

Soon enough the watercress sandwich,
  the upscale, the modish, the tasteful;
we liked what we had while we had it
  but not enough to be wistful.

A moment to stand there together
  before time to turn our back:
a scene done in diminished hues,
  a jaunty tune on the sound track:

there's a shanty in a town on a little plot of ground
where the green grass grows all around, all around
the roof so worn so badly torn it's almost falling down . . .

The green grass grows all around.

Ballad of Billy Fidenza

Someone already knows the hour,
Someone has numbered the day,
Someone for Whom there is never
Either hurry or delay.

Billy Fidenza goes by whistling
A tune from his part of town;
He pays no mind to the morning,
His fedora slanted down,

One morning in 1930,
Late summer or early fall;
Down there in Hell's Kitchen
Nobody could even recall

How many girlfriends and cardsharps
Had lost their shirts by then,
How many knifefights he had with the law,
With strangers or neighborhood men.

To some he was worse than a sharper,
And they swore he'd pay with his life;
In a dark street near the waterfront
He kept his date with a knife.

And not just one knife—three of them
Before the break of day
Suddenly came out of nowhere,
And he did not run away.

When his chest was pierced by the cold blade
His face looked none the sadder;
Billy Fidenza went to his death
As if it didn't much matter.

I think he might be pleased to know
He is still remembered in rhyme.
Forgetfulness and memory—
That's all that there is to time.

after Borges

Doctor Knows Best

Cold in her cabin in Tennessee,
she was old and poor: when her feet froze
she tried to thaw them in the fire.

"We'll have to cut them off," the doctor said
"you've got gangrene." She said no
if it came to that she'd die with her feet on.

"You've a fifty percent chance to live,
if we amputate, but with those feet:
ten percent or less."

"What do you know about living at your age."
She thought the law would help her,
but the court said

"Doctor knows best." That's what I read
in the paper, and I guess by now
they've done it, or they can:

take her down and cut her feet off,
in Tennessee. And I'm angry in California
but I bet not half as angry as she is.

For Mac McCloud and his Bemis Sonnets

That bright silverwhite cloud so black of lining
like an oldfashioned obituary card

Any happiness named or noted
acquires its edge of sorrow

Even angels were precipitated
by thinking about their own jubilation

They fell the way Saint Peter sank
when he thought "Here I am walking on water."

So what? If a poet be happy and say so
the saying comes clarified by unspoken grief

Grief and the fear of grief
when joy, too, is behovely

William Stafford

He had already posed it dozens of ways,
all of them graceful and quiet,
and when its time came round death came politely.

Bill said to Dorothy, "This was
a good day," then went away all at once—
gently, if anyone could do that gently.

O a long life, a good life, when even sorrows,
even death, could find their welcome in it.
Why then these tears.

To a Saxon Poet

Snow fallen on Northumberland has known
And forgotten every footprint that you made,
And numberless the sunsets that have grayed,
My unknown brother, between your hour and mine.
Slowly, in slow shade, you forged laborious
Metaphors of swordblades in the seas,
Of living horror hidden in the forest,
And of the solitude that dogs our days.
Where can I find your deeds, your name, your birth?
They are all long sealed in oblivion.
I'll never know you as you must have been
When you were a man like me and walked the earth.
Lone exile was the road you trudged along.
Now you are nothing but your iron song.

after Borges

Skip Stone

The lights all are out in Seeonia. At the aerodrome
the biplane that carried mail to the mainland is grounded.
Bruno Walter lays down his baton on the podium
as the Seeonia Symphony falls silent save for a lone trombone
essaying sotto voce its part from the Eroica.
Phosphorescent breakers of the Caribbean
slap softly along deserted beaches; the green glow
that runs along the length of the curl as they break in
    starlight
emits a signal of grief, for Stone is dead,
Stone the mind that conjured this island out of the void
with its language and grammar, its turbulent history,
its arts and sciences, its long quest for liberty . . .
Those revels now are ended. Stone is dead.
Well, he said, *de gustibus fatuus*.

In montibus Hawaiiensibus a creole pandanus
lashed by the ta feng (great wind or typhoon)
clings with all its roots to thin volcanic soil
while in a gentle breeze on hills above the Malacca Strait
a tall citrus lets its inedible fruit fall toward the future,
timeless deed of chaste provegetation,
and the monarch of Malaysia, after whom Stone
had prudently named that tree and its fruit,
shifts on his throne to pass a silent fart.
Stone said, *You could make marmalade.*

The paraffin lamp aglow in the deep forest has gone out,
the codices of his vast learning are quite closed up.
Our world goes ahead diminished without him,
his Flora of the Philippines left unfinished,
his campsites obscured by jungle growth or obliterated
as the jungle gives way to the century's ravages;
whole species pass unnoticed into oblivion
and what is a man, one spirited man, that we should
        remember him?
He said, *Big things come in small packages.*

Luke XXIII

Gentile or Hebrew or simply a man
Whose face is lost in time;
We shall never redeem from oblivion
The silent letters of his name.

About mercy, he knew what a bandit can know
Whom Judea nails to a cross.
Of time gone before, we can recover, now,
Nothing. During his final task,

To die crucified, he heard
Among the jibes of the people
That the man crucified next to him
Was a god, and he blurted out "Lord,

Remember me when thou comest
Into thy kingdom." The inconceivable voice
That one day will judge all beings
Promised from the terrible Cross

Paradise. They said no more
Until the end came, but history
Won't let the memory
Of that afternoon when they both died, die.

O my friends, the innocence of this friend
Of Jesus, the openness that prompted him
To ask for Paradise and to obtain it
Out of the ignominy of his chastisement

Was the same that threw him down so many times
Into bloody calamity and crimes.

after Borges

De Imagine Mundi

lama sabachthani
from the book, by memory, and in

such a fix. "Ifn you so smart
why aint you rich," et cetera. "Git down from there

and then we will believe in you har har."
Their crap game in the same book.

Prophesy, you paint the windowpanes.
Later on somebody throws a rock.

"You see, I told you there was sky out there."
A tremor, the dark, the dead rising, stone buildings

overtumbled. Facts
that save the interpretation.

Welcome Street

to the tune of Sweet Lorraine

Welcome Street
my girlfriend lives in Welcome Street
she has a double bed with striped sheets
94704 is her zip code number

I declare
it's no ordinary love affair
she keeps my tennies in her closet there
she's the one that I adore

I sure would like to ring her doorbell
sure would like to see her face
sure would like to go be welcome there
always feel so welcome in her place

she's so sweet
when I think of her my heart skips a beat
crazy bout that girl in Welcome Street
94704

Chuang Tzu and Hui Tzu

Chuang Tzu and Hui Tzu were hundreds of years old.
They flew over Galilee. Hui Tzu said,
"There goes another country boy."
"Country boy my ass," said Chuang Tzu,
"you just watch him crucifly away
up to the sky." Hui Tzu said, "You mean
crucify, not crucifly: crucify,
you asshole." Chuang Tzu said,
"Excuse me if you are mistaken."

John I, 14

Some Islamic histories have the story
Of a king who, feeling powerless in the vise
Of boring splendor, went out in disguise
And by himself to wander the poor quarter

And lose himself amidst the crush of people
Whose hands were rough and names soon forgotten.
Today, like Haroun, Emir of the Godly,
God desires to walk among the humble

And so he suckles at a mother's breast,
Just like those kin that crumble into dust,
And the whole globe shall be conveyed to him,

Air, water, morning, lily, stone and bread,
But after that—the bloody martyrdom,
The mockery, the lash, the nails, the wood.

after Borges

Near Arles, 1912: Fame

The gypsy found his friends by nightfall
and they all went on together with their bears.

He had already forgotten ever meeting a poet
on the road, whom he'd asked but who hadn't seen
the others, his lot, the ones with the bears.

And after all these years we remember him,
but we wouldn't except for the poet he met
and, also, the bears.

Texas

Here too: an endless plain
As on another continent
Where a lone cry fades
Here too the Indian, bronco, lariat

Here too all afternoon
A bird, hidden, chants memory
Above old calamities of history
Here too I read the runes

Of stars, that tune my pipe to names
That will outlast the labyrinth of days:
San Jacinto
And that other Thermopylae, the Alamo.

Here too that unknown, brief
And fretful creature, life.

after Borges

Corceca

And home she came, whereas her mother blynd
Sate in eternall night

Fairie Queene I.iii.12

She took up running to enjoy endorphins,
shuns red wine because of the histamines,
reads all the wisest magazines, stays tuned
to PBS: she spoke once on the beach
with Julia Childs. Yet in her blind heart
no peasant or savage woman in cot or hut
could be any more perplexed by superstition
than this example of a classy education.

Elizabeth Coatsworth in Hermosillo

(Hotel San Alberto, 1959)

At dawn the lady looked out her window, and saw
black patches of night lingering past her hotel:
viudas rebozudas going to early mass.
Through glass that lady looked, and she looked well.

Rancheros pintorescos with their horsedrawn carts
were bringing produce to market by first light;
with a sound that rang to her like History
their iron wheels roared on the cobblestone street.

And the *lechero*, the *tamalero*, the early *paletero*
passed singly, each with a differing cry.
She saw skylark schoolboys, but for one
who benched himself with his lesson: "*¡Ay*

menso!" *le gritaban los demas*,
but she didn't hear it, or need to.
She could see more than most of us
because she knew what She knew

and though she knew no Spanish
her New England voice was so clear
any clerk could understand it;
and not just that, they liked Her.

It's my language that wants to be insolent,
and finds appalling ways to be true
and cuts like broken glass from a window
and won't fit: like this I'm telling you.

Geneva, 1916

A glance along the table,
light words, heady laughter,
the possibly deliberate
pressure of an ankle,

a possible innuendo
in clever things she said:
one thing led to another,
and she led him to her bed.

It seemed to him a conquest
though she were oh so willing;
but after a night with her
he woke up in the morning

to find that she had done it
as a favor to his father.
She, his father's mistress.
He felt "unstable as water,"

like Reuben in the Bible.
An atavistic sheen
undid the sexual debut
of this son from the Argentine

but gave him, as a poet,
a thought to write about:
whether all our deeds are darkened
by the shadow of a doubt;

who is, in any action,
the actor, who the author?
If you do what another has done,
are you the same, or the other?

Proteus

Shepherd of seal flock
gifted with second sight
he would hoard seercraft,
utter ambiguous oracle

Lonely on Pharos beach
his daughter it was, betrayed him
Eidothea
gave advice to a Greek

Gave also ambrosia
so they could jump him, hang on,
twist out of him tidings
despite seal-hide aroma

War-weary Achaians scattering for home
for all the good it did, any of them

(adapted from an abandoned translation of Borges)

Midgarthormr

Endless the sea. Endless the green sea-creature,
world-generating snake whose length is curled—
green ocean and green serpent—against the world
in a circle, like the world. The mouth reaches
to bite the tail stretching from far away,
from the other side. Within its strong constrictions
we live—in storm, deep shadow, brilliant day,
echo and noise, reflections of reflections.
And it is the amphisbæna. Forevermore
its many eyes regard its many eyes
without the slightest horror. Each head, likewise,
grossly sniffs out the weapons and spoils of war.
In Iceland it was dreamt. In storms and gales
the open sea caught sight of it, and knew fear.
Out of the deep one day it will reappear
with the curst ship made out of corpses' nails.
Its vast shadow, unthinkable, will tower
over the pallid earth that frightful day
of giant wolves, magestic agony,
the unspeakable twilight of the gods' last hour.
Its image, imagined, soils everyone.
I saw it in a nightmare, toward dawn.

after Borges

Mister Nixon Making History

When the ghost emperor from Gold Mountain
journeyed in state to the Central Kingdom,
TV crews were perched on platforms
by the airport road. Like bonfires set
to bring the news when Troy had fallen,
they relayed photo trophies home:
that Chinese limousine approaching,
passing, and then from nearer in
approaching, passing—all by itself
on a two lane road between bare elms
with nobody, not one soul to witness
until, when it entered the Forbidden City,
an old man on a bicycle, who didn't
turn his head nor seem to notice,
pedalled across an almost empty square.

A Pantoum for Anselm Kiefer

A book made of lead floats over fields
Of tar, iron, shellac, clay, lead, and dirt;
The artist proclaims himself sacrificed, martyred,
Forgotten, insistent, unyielding.

Of tar, iron, shellac, clay, lead and dirt
The artist fabricates books without words.
Forgotten, insistent, unyielding,
He claims to be conscience and is despised.

The artist fabricates books without words,
Iron skis, a lead ladder, a furrow of milk in a field.
He claims to be conscience, and is despised
In his own country, a prophet abroad.

Iron skis, a lead ladder, a furrow of milk in a field:
All these heavy things never would work.
In his own country a prophet, abroad
He must already be a millionaire.

All these heavy things never would work
If it weren't for energy, presence, patience, Art.
He must already be a millionaire,
Everyone knows he is a recluse.

If it weren't for energy, presence, patience, Art,
Nobody would care about his conscience.
Everyone knows he is a recluse
But something does need to be announced.

Nobody would care about his conscience,
The artist proclaims—himself sacrificed, martyred—
But something does need to be announced.
A book made of lead floats over fields.

A Fresco at San Fortunato, Todi

in gremio matris sapientia patris

Dust now the eye that led, the hand that traced
this mother and huge child; dust too the donors
depicted here small scale as worshipers;
the heat and damp of seven centuries
have crumbled plaster, have almost erased
this fresco memory. The child's right hand
was raised in a gesture signifying Power;
his left may once have held an orb; Wisdom
and Power were shown made One by Love.
And still, from its decay, this witnesses:
though wisdom lose its edge, be laughed to scorn,
though power corrupt itself by its own force,
the love that moved that hand, that thrilled that eye,
is a true gift given this and all the worlds.

Dick Barnes identified "Hatauva" as a "Serrano Indian vil-
lage in the San Bernardino mountains, ancestral home of
the coyote moiety of the tribe," and Benjamin Morongo as a
full-blooded Serrano who as a child "saw the spring and the
marks in the ground where the people . . . danced around the
funeral pyre of the demiurge Kukitat." More of the story can
be found near the end of "A Visit to Lonesome John: Autumn
Coming."

"Malleys" in "The Longing of the Soul for Absence" were
"great steam locomotives with two sets of pistons and drivers
. . . that used to shuttle between San Bernardino and Victorville
helping trains over Cajon Pass."

Of "Rakestraw Coyne and Boyle," Dick Barnes wrote, "Rub-
ber seeds smuggled out of Brazil by a dishonest British civil
servant were stolen by a rascally customs officer in Honduras:
'When I find someone rich enough to buy them, he'll be smart
enough to know what they are.' Pursued by the civil servant
who was himself pursued by a mysterious Brazilian, the cus-
toms officer joined a group of other scoundrels driving stolen
cattle from the 'cow countries' of Southern California to the
gold fields in the north." "A short job of work for Bertie
Rodgers" was the few months in the late forties that the Irish
poet, W. R. Rodgers, worked for the Dunlop Tyre and Rub-
ber Company, composing ad slogans (none of which were

used, being thought too racy). Rodgers taught for a while in Claremont and he and Dick Barnes were great friends.

In "A Lake on the Earth: The Swarm," Bicycle Lake is a dry lake on the Mojave desert.

Bert Meyers, to whom "Learning Death" is dedicated, was a fine poet who lived in Claremont for many years, teaching at Pitzer, and died, much too early, of lung cancer.

In "Example and Admonition," "the Chou I book" is the *I Ching*.

Some readers have assumed that "Willie Boy" was inspired by the film of the same name; in fact, it is based on old newspaper accounts of the actual murder and pursuit.

In "September, 1950," CMC is Claremont Men's College (since renamed Claremont McKenna).

"*Con los Hombres a Robar, con los Cabrones ni al Agua*" (which means, roughly, "[Go] with men even to rob, but with bastards not even to water") is the last of a sequence of five poems called "A Meditation on the Desert Fathers."

A "Santana," or Santa Ana, is a warm dry wind that blows through the passes and canyons of the coastal ranges of Southern California, usually in early winter. It is a very strong wind, between 35 and 50 knots; sometimes gusts are greater than 100 knots.

"Erles," wrote Dick Barnes, "is a word used by the author of *The Cloud of Unknowing* to signify the sweetness that can be experienced by contemplatives while still in this life: it translates the Latin *arrha*, earnest money." And he goes on: "Azrael, Uriel, Zadkiel, Gabriel, Annael, Michael and Raphael are the planets of the old astronomy (Saturn, Mars, Jupiter, the moon, Venus, Mercury, and the sun respectively) by their Arabic names."

It would help a reader trying to get to the bottom of "An Old Story" to recognize the three legends that are used. The Sleeping Beauty is obvious; Sir Bertilak is the Green Knight and one should know at least the story of *Sir Gawain and the Green Knight*; Xantippe (or Xanthippe) is the shrewish wife of Socrates, a shrew in the legend at any rate, and Dick Barnes is alluding here to one of her rages, in which she throws a pot of hot water— sometimes it's a pot of urine—at Socrates, who responds, "After the thunder comes the rain." This beautiful, anguished and difficult poem is one of his most deeply personal.

For "Mac McCloud and his Bemis sonnets": Mac McCloud is the pen name of Mac McClain, the "guru back then" of "Bill Munsen, An Elegy" (p. 62), who graduated from Pomona in 1955, a year after Dick Barnes. "Bemis" refers to the Bemis Center of Contemporary Arts in Omaha, Nebraska, where McClain, a well-known potter and sculptor, was a resident artist in 1991.

"lama sabachthani": Christ's words on the Cross, "why hast thou forsaken me?" (Matthew 27:46, Mark 15:34. See also Psalms 22:1)

"Chuang Tzu and Hui Tzu" are thinkers who lived in the 4th century BCE. Hui Tzu, or Hui Shih, was a logical philosopher; they were good friends despite the great difference between their modes of thought, which Waley describes as "intellectuality as opposed to imagination."

In "Near Arles, 1912: Fame," the poet who has made us remember the gypsy is Ezra Pound; see his poem, "The Gypsy," in *Lustra*, in which Pound speaks a little scornfully of having seen all too many gypsies but no bears.

"Corceca" (blind heart) is the name of Superstition in *The Faerie Queene*.

"San Jacinto" was a twenty-minute battle, fought soon after the disaster at the Alamo, which resulted in a rout of the Mexican army, the capture of Santa Anna, and Texan independence.

The Spanish in "Elizabeth Coatsworth in Hermosillo" is fairly simple, but for the reader with none, *"viudas rebozudas"* are widows wrapped in their shawls; *"rancheros pintorescos"* are picturesque rustics; the *"lechero," "tamalero"* and *"paletero"* are the milkman, the tamale man and the local yokel, respectively; and the fourth stanza begins, "'Ah, stupid!' cried the others."

If the reader has not already guessed, the young man in "Geneva, 1916" is the 17-year-old Borges. This story is probably a true one.

Midgard (middle world) in Norse mythology is the world of human beings, and the "amphisbæna" is an immense serpent with two heads that lies deep in the ocean and, one head biting the other, encirles the entire world—all of us are caught in its coils. But Dick Barnes noted that the amphisbæna is out of Lucan's *Pharsalia* and not really the same as the Midgarthormr, the Old Norse world serpent.

"Mister Nixon Making History" refers, of course, to his famous visit to China in February of 1972; there were no crowds at the Beijing airport nor on the road to the Forbidden City, once the emperor's palace, later Mao's.

The epigraph to the last poem, "A Fresco at San Fortunato, Todi," means "the father's wisdom in the mother's lap (or bosom)."